# The Amazing Quilling Projects
## Beautiful And Creative Ideas To Start Quilling For Beginners

Copyright © 2021

All rights reserved.

**DEDICATION**

The author and publisher have provided this e-book to you for your personal use only. You may not make this e-book publicly available in any way. Copyright infringement is against the law. If you believe the copy of this e-book you are reading infringes on the author's copyright, please notify the publisher at: https://us.macmillan.com/piracy

# Contents

The Basics .................................................................................... 1

    What is Paper Quilling? ........................................................ 1

    The History of Paper Quilling ............................................... 1

    Materials and Tools Required for Paper Quilling .............. 2

    How to Make Your Paper Quilling Water Resistant with Sealant ................................................................................ 11

    How to Choose the Perfect Paper or Cut Your Own ....... 17

Basic Paper Quilling Shapes Instructions ................................ 25

5 Paper Quilling Patterns for Beginners .................................. 49

    Paper Quilled Monogram ................................................... 49

    Paper Quilled Teardrop Vase .............................................. 56

    Paper Quilled Flower Cake ................................................. 62

    Paper Quilling Flower Pendant .......................................... 65

Create A Quilled Paper Flower Photo Frame! .................. 75

# The Basics

## What is Paper Quilling?

Quilling is the art of manipulating and arranging small strips of paper into detailed designs. Depending on the desired shape and appearance, it can be rolled, looped, twisted, and curled. Glue is used to secure the paper strips into place.

Paper quilling is a decorative art and is known for things like fancy flourishes and florals. Because of this reputation, it's commonly used on things like greeting cards, boxes, jewelry, and more. But with its recent surge in popularity, it's also seen in advertising campaigns and pieces you might find in an art gallery.

## The History of Paper Quilling

Like many forms of craft, paper quilling can trace its origins back hundreds of years to at least the 15th century (maybe earlier). It is believed to have been created by French and Italian nuns and used to decorate religious objects in an effort to save money. The filigree was fashioned to simulate carved ivory and wrought iron—two very costly details. When the paper quilling was gilded, it was hard to distinguish from metal, making it a good option for struggling churches.

Paper quilling had its heyday in England during the 18th century. It, in addition to embroidery, was considered a "proper pastime" for young women and was taught in boarding schools, as well as to "ladies of leisure" because it was seen as not too "taxing" for them. Quilling's influence spread to the United States, but the practice waned by the 19th century; there are relatively few examples of paper quilling during this time.

Paper quilling has had a renaissance as creatives have rediscovered the techniques. They are using them in traditional ways, but many, have given the curling and bending of paper a modern twist. She uses the material like you would strokes of paint; her folded pieces resemble Impressionist artwork.

# Materials and Tools Required for Paper Quilling

Beginning quilling can be accomplished using only strips of paper, a toothpick, knitting needle or similar object, and some glue. If you get bitten by the quilling bug, you can invest in proper quilling tools to make your job that much easier.

**Materials**

*Quilling Paper*

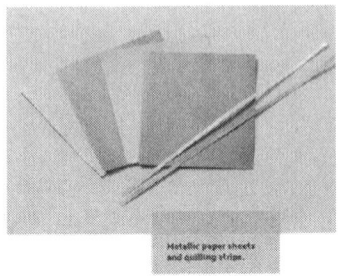

Metallic paper sheets and quilling strips.

Quilling paper is readily available as precut strips, and some colors can be purchased in sheet form. In general, quilling paper is a bit thicker and softer to the touch than regular printer paper. The weight of the strips featured in The Art of Quilling Paper Jewelry, for example, is generally 100 or 120 gsm (grams per square meter). In comparison, printer paper weighs 80 to 90 gsm, while cardstock is 170 gsm and higher.

**Precut Strips**

Whatever type of quilling strips you use, expect them to be accurately cut with a width that is exactly the same from end to end. If using archival supplies is important to you, buy strips that are labeled acid-free. Some paper brands are slightly heavier than others, and some colors are heavier within a single brand. Each type handles slightly differently, but all are cut with the grain to ensure smooth rolling. Quilling strips are usually reasonably priced, and it is fun to experiment with different brands to determine your favorites. Since I began quilling fifteen years ago, I have used many different types of strips from online suppliers in the United States and the United Kingdom. All have proven to be high-quality strips that are evenly cut and richly colored.

## *Metallic Quilling Strips*

All of the projects in The Art of Quilling Paper Jewelry call for standard 1/8" (3 mm) wide strips with a gold, silver, or copper edge to give each piece the look of fine jewelry. While 1/8" (3 mm) may sound impossibly narrow, fear not! With practice, your fingers will grow accustomed to handling it fairly quickly.

The pendant and earring designs in my book are predominately made with metallic-edge black or ivory papers, but there is no need to limit yourself to just two choices. Metallic-edge papers can be ordered in a wide range of colors from at least three online retailers in the United States who import them from England. The British paper comes in packages of thirty 1/8" x 17" (3 mm x 43 cm) strips, which is enough to make several pieces of jewelry. (Note: The length of your quilling strip will directly affect the finished size of your quilled shapes.) Additionally, Dutch metallic-edge strips measuring 1/8" x 19." (3 mm x 49.5 cm) are also available through a U.S. supplier and come twenty-five to a package.

If you want the look of metallic edge strips but prefer a more, subtle shine, try A Touch of Gold and A Touch of Silver quilling paper. This type of American made metallic-edge strip is available in single color packages of fifty 1/8" x 24" (3 mm x

61 cm) strips, as well as packs of 100 multicolor 1/8" x 20–24" (3 mm x 51–61 cm) strips.

L to R: Needle tool teardrop coils made with 5" (12.5 cm), 4" (10 cm), and 3" (7.5 cm) strips.

(Additional details on working with colorful quilling strips and paper sheets can be found in The Art of Quilling Paper Jewelry.)

**Tools**

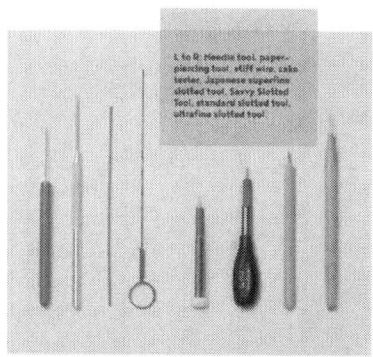

L to R: Needle tool, paper-piercing tool, stiff wire, cake tester, Japanese superfine slotted tool, Savvy Slotted Tool, standard slotted tool, ultrafine slotted tool

### *Slotted Tool*

With the easy-to-use slotted tool, a paper strip is slid into a slot that immediately grips the end, allowing for the smooth rotation of the tool with a relaxed hand. The trade-off is that the slot leaves a small crimp in the center of the coil. It's certainly not the end of the world, but sometimes a crimp is frowned upon by quilling purists. That said, I have yet to meet anyone who upon seeing a piece of slotted-tool jewelry for the first time is dismayed by the coil crimps. Instead, they are too busy exclaiming they can't believe the beautiful object is made of paper! I suggest learning to quill with both tools to determine your preference.

### *Slotted Tool Choices*

It is important to note that not all slotted tools are alike. The standard slotted tool is a strong workhorse, but it leaves a considerably larger crimp than a fine slotted tool. A Japanese superfine slotted tool has a very small slot and a shaft that rotates smoothly. The crimp it produces can barely be detected. Common sense will tell you to not overstress the fine prongs by rolling the paper so tightly that the crimp is torn off, a practice some quillers employ with success when using a standard slotted tool.

A tool called the Savvy Slotted Tool is similar in design to the Japanese tool, but it has an ergonomic handle and the slot produces a slightly larger crimp. A fourth type of slotted tool has an ultrafine slot that is not set close to the handle, making it difficult to gain rolling leverage. That said, if it is the only tool you have access to as a new quiller, you may learn to quill beautifully with it.

**Needle Tool**

With this tool, a strip is rolled around a needle. It takes a bit of extra effort to learn to quill with a needle tool, but the advantage is that it produces a coil with a tiny, perfectly round center. The disadvantage is that it takes more time to learn to quill with a needle tool, but with practice, you can become a pro at rolling smooth, even coils.

**Needle Tool Substitutes**

Any slim, sturdy wire can take the place of a needle tool. In fact, my first quilling tool was a cake tester, a stiff wire that is inserted into a cake to see if the batter is baked all the way through. A cocktail stick (round toothpick), a doll-making or upholstery needle, or even a corsage or hatpin can be substituted as well. Of course, a true needle tool with a handle will be more comfortable to grip, but these stand-ins will give you the opportunity to try your hand at needle-tool rolling.

***Note:*** Your choice of quilling tool will be most noticeable in the center of spirals. In the examples shown, you'll see slotted tools leave a slight crimp in the paper end at the center of the spiral, which the needle tool spiral has no crimp.

Coils made with different tools. L to R: Japanese superfine slotted tool, standard slotted tool, needle tool.

**Glues & fixatives**

***White Glue vs. Clear Glue***

Ask ten quillers to name their glue of choice and you'll likely get ten different answers. Elmer's School Glue, Aleene's Original Tacky Glue, and Sobo Premium Craft and Fabric Glue are names of white glues you'll frequently hear. I prefer to use a clear glue, such as Martha Stewart Crafts All-Purpose Gel Adhesive. (Elmer's

Clear School Glue is another option.) Unlike white glue, clear glues do not quickly thicken and develop a skin when exposed to air on a glue palette.

***Safety note:*** I always look for glues and fixatives that are nontoxic and free of fumes.

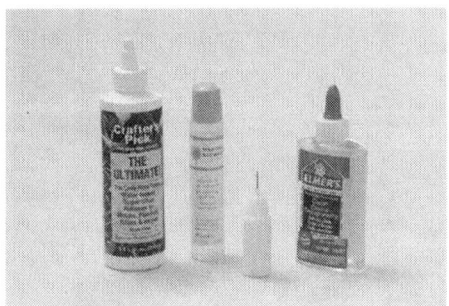

### Acid-Free Glue

Acidic glues can discolor paper and cause it to become brittle over time, so I prefer to use glues that are acid-free. Martha Stewart Crafts All-Purpose Gel Adhesive is an example of an acid-free clear glue. Aleene's makes an acid-free white Tacky Glue.

### Adhering to Metal or Plastic

When gluing quilled pieces to a nonporous surface, such as metal or plastic, Crafter's Pick The Ultimate is my adhesive of choice because it securely holds coils and scrolls in place, dries clear, and is durable and nontoxic. I prefer to place a small dollop of glue on a palette (a recycled plastic container lid works really well) and dip from it sparingly with the tip of a ball-head pin, paper-piercing tool, or T-pin. This way, I can easily control the amount of glue I use and keep my hand relaxed, because there is no squeezing motion as there is with a plastic bottle.

**Fixatives**

Truth be told, I rarely use a fixative on quilled jewelry. I prefer the look of natural paper rather than the plastic shine of glossy fixatives, not to mention there is always the chance that moisture in a spray or brush-on product will cause coil centers to swell. However, for an extra layer of protection, especially if you live in a warm, humid climate, you can apply a protective coating, such as Liquitex Professional Matte Varnish. (Apply a thin layer or two using a small paintbrush or repurposed makeup brush.) This type of varnish is nontoxic, virtually odor-free, and will not significantly change the look of quilling paper. I recommend applying it only to the back of a jewelry piece because it will dull the bright shine of metallic-edge paper.

If you've taken notes through this post you'll know all you need to get started quilling paper jewelry is 1/8" quilling paper, a needle or slotted quilling tool (though a tooth pick will work in a pinch!), and your choice of acid-free glue. I bet you have those in your jewelry studio already!

# How to Make Your Paper Quilling Water Resistant with Sealant

First up, PPA (Perfect Paper Adhesive). PPA is a glue, a sealant, and a topcoat. It provides a very water resistant layer to your paper quilling. PPA is my absolute favorite glue for paper quilling.

To use as a sealant, either dip your brush into some PPA or squeeze some PPA onto your brush from your glue bottle. Paint the PPA onto your quilling piece on one side. You will notice that it is white looking. But don't worry, it dries perfectly clear and also soaks into the paper, so it won't leave clumps. When one side has dried, you can flip it over and do the same to the other side. When the second side has dried, put another layer on, this time dabbing your brush into all the crooks and crannies to cover all surfaces. The better you cover your surfaces, the more sturdy and water resistant your piece will be. In these photos I used PPA to seal this butterfly earring:

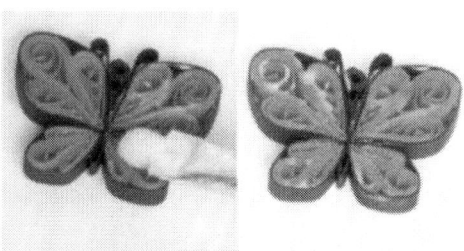

Another nice feature of PPA is that it comes in matte or gloss. The matte has a very matte finish, nice for when you don't want your paper quilling to look shiny at all, but still want that sturdy and water resistant finish. When you use PPA as a sealant, the color of your paper will stay exactly the same, nice when you don't want to risk a sealer that may change the shade of your paper. The gloss is a very nice shiny look.

Next up, liquid matte sealant – this is the sealant that I most commonly use for my paper quilled jewelry because it works very well.

It comes in a little jar with a flip top lid (like in the photo above, not in the photos below). It is called matte sealer, but if you use several layers your finished piece will have a bit of a shine (but not as shiny as a gloss finish sealant). If you just use one layer it will be matte. This sealant is very useful for many crafts! I've often painted it over paper mache that has been painted with poster paints which helps seal the paint so it doesn't chip and also makes it water resistant. But of course I mostly use it for paper quilling!

To use all you do is dip your brush into it and paint it onto your piece. For most quilling you'll want to paint one side, let it dry, paint the other side and let it dry, and lastly paint all the crevices and let it dry. The reason you want to do one side at a time and then the crevices is that if you put too much sealant on all at once your piece can get soggy and out of shape. By using several layers (allowing it to dry between layers) it prevents this from happening. This sealant is white, but it quickly soaks in and dries to a clear matte finish. Because this sealant is liquid you could also pour it into a small spray bottle and spray it onto your pieces. I did this for a long time, but now I prefer the painting method because it doesn't waste some of the sealant. But if you are doing a large surface area, then the spraying method works great! For solid pieces of quilling you can also just dip the piece into the sealant, dab off the excess with a tissue, and lay to dry on a plastic surface.

When you use this liquid matte sealer on your paper quilling you will notice that it makes the shade of your paper just a TINY bit darker. I have not found this to be a problem at all, but just wanted to point it out. When the sealer soaks into the paper you can see the color difference. Also, if you want to make sure your piece is water resistant you definitely want to do at least two complete coats of this sealant. Because it soaks into the paper so much, sometimes one layer is just not enough. Your piece will still be sturdy and mostly water resistant, but there is definitely a better result with at least two complete layers. You will notice as you put on the second layer that it does not soak in as quickly as the first layer.

The third type of sealant I use is Crystal Coat Glaze (find it here at Custom Quilling or here on Amazon). It gives a clear glossy finish! This is my favorite sealant to use when I make pieces that are inset such as this one below. Just glue your pieces into the inset pendant base (use the crystal coat glaze as your glue as well) and then squeeze a layer of crystal coat glaze over the whole thing. It will appear to look 3D and a cloudy color, but will flatten out as it dries to fill in all the crevices and be clear, shiny, and hard! Allow to dry for at least a couple days for a hard finish, at least in a tropical climate like it is here! If you use the crystal coat glaze for this purpose, one tube will usually last between 2-4 pendants (each pack comes with three bottles). *it now comes in either a three pack of little tubes or a new 2 oz. bottle! You could also use PPA glossy for this purpose.

Here I am using crystal coat glaze as a topcoat for these quilled pieces. They have already been dipped into the liquid matte sealant and left to dry. But I wanted to give a final coat that was glossy. I just squeeze a bit of the glaze onto my paintbrush and paint it onto one side of the piece. After it dries I'll do the other side and then the sides. I also often put my earrings onto their earring hooks, then add the crystal coat glaze to all sides at once and hang to dry on my earring rack.

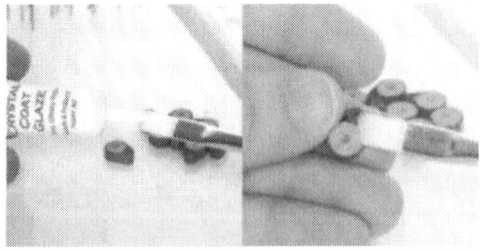

Instead of painting the glaze on you can also just squeeze it on. This has a nice effect because it gives a bit of a thicker coat. You can hold it in your hand to do this, or lay it on a plastic surface. Make sure one side is completely dry before doing the second side! You can use crystal coat glaze as your only sealant, but I usually use it on top of the liquid matte sealer so that I don't have to use as much crystal coat glaze, unless I am using it for an inset pendant as seen above. The reason I do this is that it is a bit more expensive than the other options and works just as well if just used as a topcoat over another sealant.

So there are three of the types of sealant that I currently use. With any of them, make sure you rinse your paintbrush completely immediately after using the sealants so they don't dry onto your brush. If they do dry onto your brush, just soak in soapy hot water to try and get off as much as the sealant as you can, but you may have to replace your brush anyway.

# How to Choose the Perfect Paper or Cut Your Own

Picking out a type of paper that will work for your quilling project can actually be trickier than cutting it yourself. When you buy paper from quilling suppliers, they do the choosing for you. When you go your own way, the paper selection is up to you. So let's start off with tips on how to choose the best paper, before we get into how to cut it.

**Choosing the Weight**

The weight of the paper (i.e. the thickness) has a huge impact not only on how the finished project looks, but also on how easy it is to make. Commercial strips usually come in writing weight, text weight or card stock. Play around with all those options, so you can feel comfortable when it's time to make a paper selection on your own.

**Writing Weight**

Writing weight paper (about 20 pounds) is the lightest kind. It's similar in thickness to the paper you'd typically use in your printer, and it's useful for more traditional or delicate quilling. It tends to tear easily if you ask too much of it.

**Text Weight**

This paper is heavier (around 60 to 80 pounds) and is usually best for modern quilling projects like jewelry. A heavier paper like this kind can stand up to stretching and extra manipulation. But if you're going for a traditional quilling look, it's better to stick with a lighter weight.

## Card Stock

This weight category is typically used for quilling typography projects and outlining in mosaics. It varies from 60-pound bristol weight up to 110-pound cover stock or higher. When working with card stock, remember that the heavier the weight, the less quilling-friendly the paper will be. You can still coil and roll up bristol weight card stock with a quilling tool, but cover stock is too thick to fit into a tool and would crack when rolled. Still, the heavier weights are an excellent choice for straight and gently curved lines.

## Selecting a Finish

There's no end to the varieties of paper out there, in pretty much any finish you can imagine. But not all finishes work well for quilling projects, so it's best to know what you're getting into.

### *Metallic Paper*

Metallic paper definitely looks fantastic, and most kinds are available in a heavier text weight. But while metallic paper is easy to cut at home, the glossy finish isn't as easy to glue; you'll need a bit more drying time, not to mention patience.

### *One-Sided Paper*

If you've ever walked down the scrapbook aisle of your local craft store, you've probably been tempted to quill with some of the fabulous paper there. One-sided paper, for instance, can be an excellent choice for some projects, but remember that in quilling, it's only the edge of the paper that shows. Since one-sided paper is usually printed or backed on white, it's not so ideal for coils, but it does work well for outlining a shape.

**Specialty Paper**

Specialty papers can be lots of fun to use, but some are better than others for cutting at home. The paper in the image above, made from genuine cherry wood, is beautiful but a little tough to cut. Consider the specific qualities of the paper you're planning to use when you're choosing your cutting surface and tools — because safety first!

**Vat-Dyed Colored Paper**

Fact: Vat-dyed paper is the easiest to cut, the easiest to quill and the easiest to find at your local store. Colored paper can be wonderful for most quilling projects. Just be sure to choose acid-free, colorfast paper. After all, quilling is a time-consuming project, and you want your masterpieces to last!

**Finding the Correct Length**

One last thing to consider before stepping into the studio is the length of your paper. The standard 8.5-by-11-inch size is ubiquitous in stores, but most quilling patterns use strips that are 17 inches or longer. If you can find the larger size, you'll have a slightly easier time following a pattern. If not, don't sweat it. A little glue is all you need to get the right length.

**How to Make Your Own Quilling Paper**

# The Amazing Quilling Projects

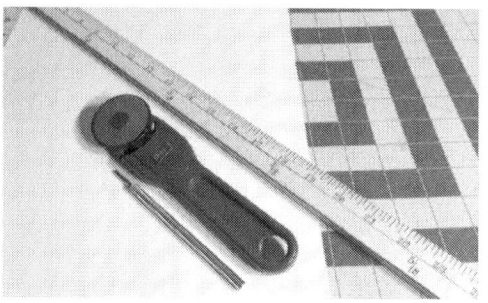

## *What You Need*

- ❖ Self-healing mat or appropriate cutting surface
- ❖ Ruler or yard stick
- ❖ Craft knife or rotary cutter
- ❖ Paper of choice

1. Square Up Your Edges

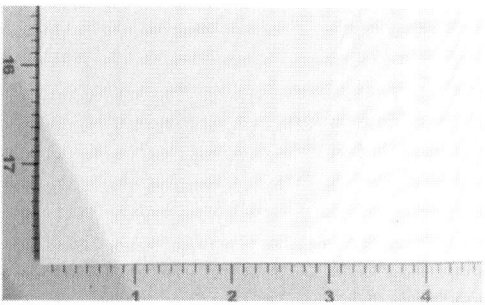

Using the ruler on your self-healing mat, square up the edges on the left-hand side of your paper sheet.

**2.** Trim Away the Excess

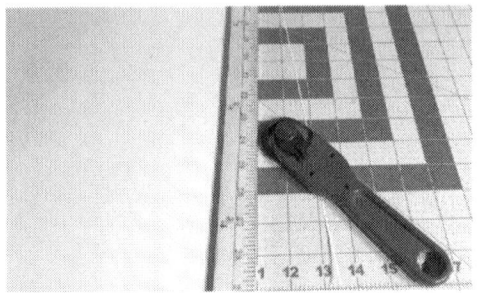

Use your yard stick to square up the opposite side of your paper. Sheets are almost never cut to perfection, so you'll need to trim off the excess before you start cutting. A rotary cutter can be safer than a utility knife, but use whichever one you prefer.

**3.** Line it Up

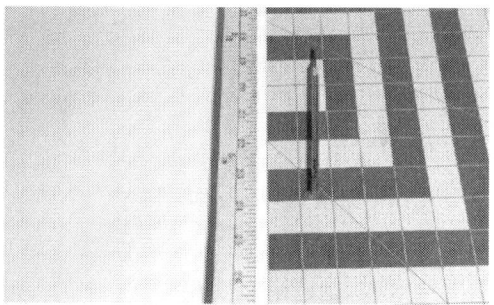

Holding your paper securely in place, move your yard stick to the left. The preset markings on the self-healing mat will give you the width you want when you cut.

**4.** Cut Your Strip

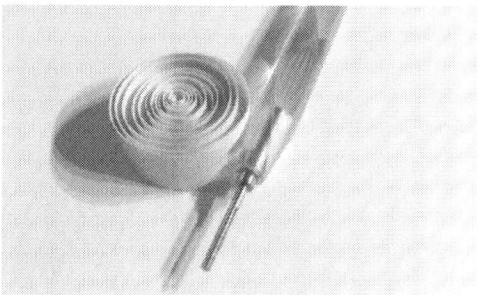

If you're cutting with a rotary tool, you might find it easiest to begin at the bottom and move upward. With a utility knife, the opposite can be true. Whichever tool you're using, lean heavily into the yard stick with your body weight and hand to avoid slipping as you cut.

And there's your self-cut quilling paper! Now that you know how to make your own, repeat this process to create as many strips as you need.

# Basic Paper Quilling Shapes Instructions

Here are the basic shapes that are frequently adopted in quilling. The step-by-step instructions will help you to create each shape. Once you have mastered these, you will be able to create almost any quilled design!

**What You Need**

- A slotted quilling tool
- Quilling glue in a needle-tip bottle
- Scissors
- Tweezers
- Package of quilling paper strips — for beginners, I recommend ¼-inch wide (it's easy to grip and manipulate); once you've mastered the basic shapes, you may prefer narrower strips. Cut the strips 8½-inches long for this tutorial.

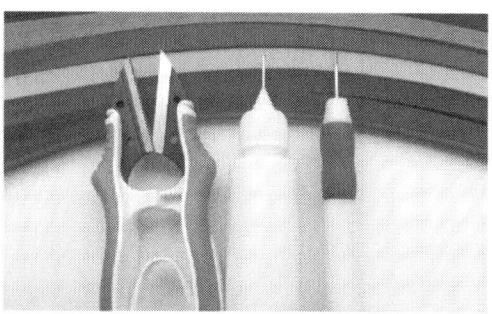

**Open and Closed Coils**

Simple circles are the basis for most other shapes you'll create.

*1. Insert Paper into the Tool*

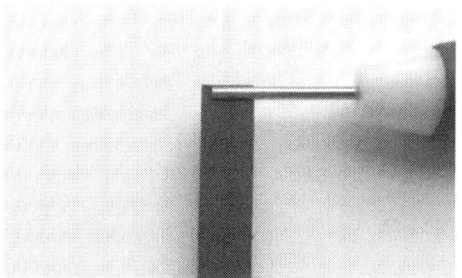

Insert a piece of quilling paper into the slot of your quilling tool; try to line up the edge of the paper with the edge of the slot as perfectly as you can. A slotted tool will naturally leave a small crimp in the center of your coil. If you'd like the crimp to be more visible, allow the paper to hang slightly over the edge.

2. *Start Rollin'*

Roll the tool with your dominant hand either towards your body or away from it (whichever feels most comfortable), while holding the strip taut with your other hand.

3. *Glue It*

For a closed coil: When you're almost done coiling, place a dab of glue near the end of the strip and roll to complete. You don't want it to expand after you remove it from the tool.

For an open coil: Finish the coil, then remove it from the tool and allow it to expand. Once it has fully expanded, add a dab of glue and press the strip down carefully to secure.

**Teardrop**

Make an open coil, then place it between the thumb and forefinger of your non-dominant hand. Arrange the inside coils evenly or however you'd like.

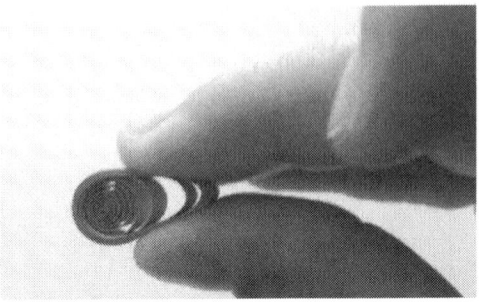

With your dominant hand, pinch the paper where you want the point to be to create a teardrop shape.

*Teardrop Variations*

Basic shapes can be manipulated to create even more shapes. The teardrop is an excellent example of this.

By slightly curving the teardrop around your thumb as you shape it, you can create a subtle shift in form without compromising the center coils. To exaggerate this effect, you can wrap the teardrop around your quilling tool or another cylindrical object.

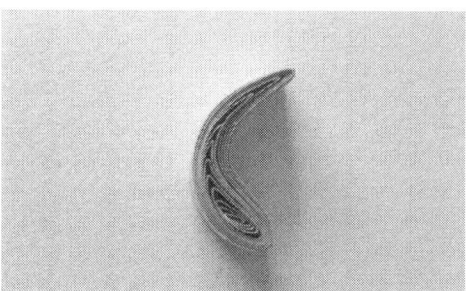

For a more obvious curved shape throughout, press the shape around your quilling tool. From here, you can easily create a paisley shape.

The Amazing Quilling Projects

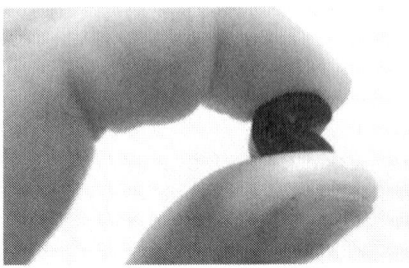

You can curl the shape from the point to the base by rolling it between your fingers.

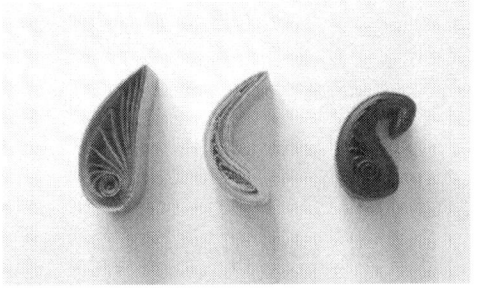

So many shapes!

**Marquis**

First make a teardrop shape, then pinch the opposite end as well.

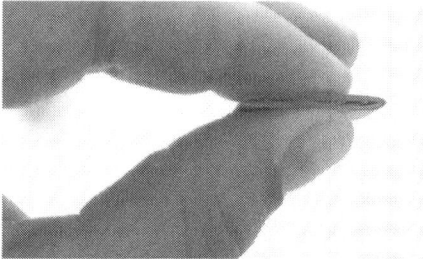

The final shape will be determined by how much you pinch or press the the coil together and where you place its center.

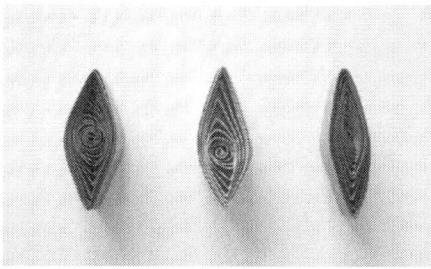

Play around with different placements and pressure to create lots of marquis versions.

**Tulip**

First make a marquis shape, then turn the shape on its side and pinch a center peak with your fingers.

**Slug**

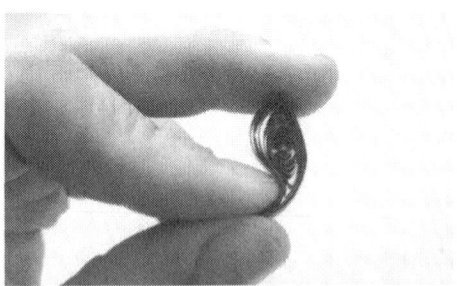

Start with a marquis, then wrap one end around the tip of your finger or a quilling tool.

Do the same to the other end but in the opposite direction. Looks pretty for a slug, doesn't it!

**Square or Diamond**

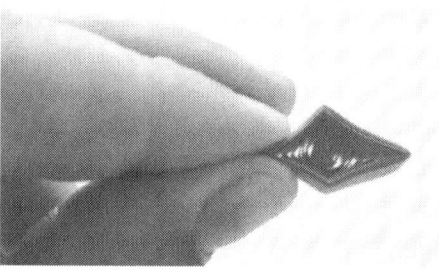

Create a marquis shape, then rotate it 90 degrees and pinch both sides again. This will create a diamond shape.

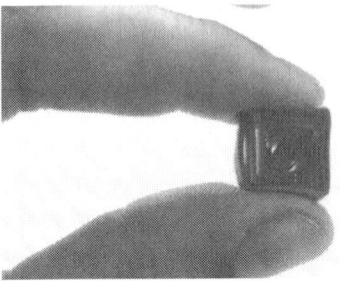

If you want to continue on to making a square, gently open up the shape between your fingers.

**Square Variations**

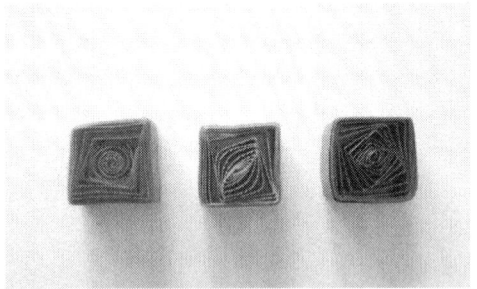

By playing around with how much of each corner you choose to pinch when creating your square, you can get very different results.

Above left: By applying pressure to the outside corners, you can create a square with a rounded center.

Above center: This was made by completely pressing the open coil together on one side, then opening it up and pinching just the corners on the opposite side. Above right: This got its unique center by completely pressing down the coil on both turns.

Yet another variation on the square: You can make these by applying pressure to the outside structure with your fingers or the stem of your quilling tool.

**Rectangle**

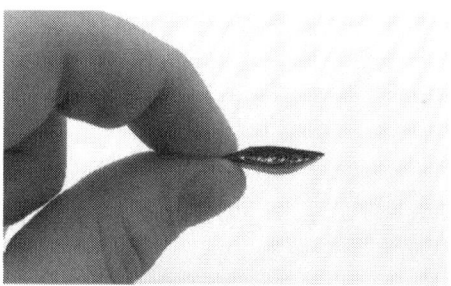

If you can make a square, you can make a rectangle. The difference is in how much you rotate the marquis shape before pinching additional angles.

Rotate it only slightly (rather than 90 degrees) before pinching and then open the shape to reveal the perfect rectangle.

**Rectangle Variations**

Alternately, you can create a quadrilateral shape by making your four corners at uneven intervals.

This shape is especially useful when you're making quilled paper mosaics and you need to fill in an odd space.

**Semi-Circle**

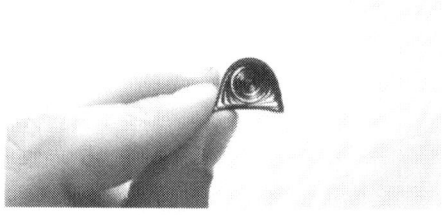

Start with an open coil, then pinch two corners while leaving the paper above them round. You can also do this by pressing an open coil onto a hard surface like a table and sliding your fingers down the sides carefully. Try both methods to see which suits you best.

The Amazing Quilling Projects

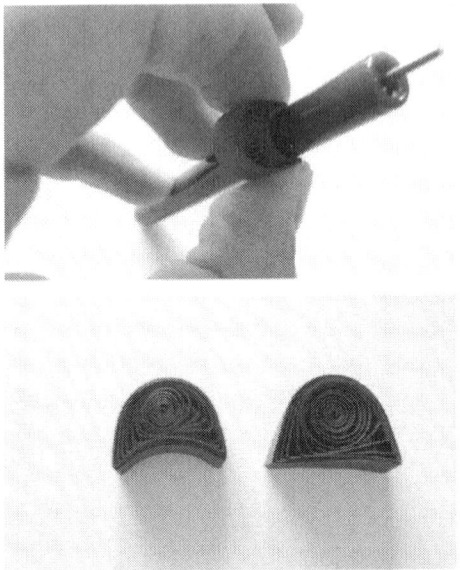

Curving the straight edge of the shape will allow you to turn a semi-circle into more of a crescent moon shape.

**Triangle**

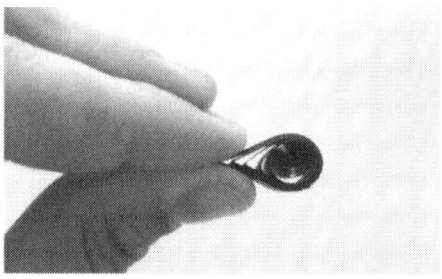

Make a teardrop shape, then pinch two additional angles using either your fingers or the tabletop method.

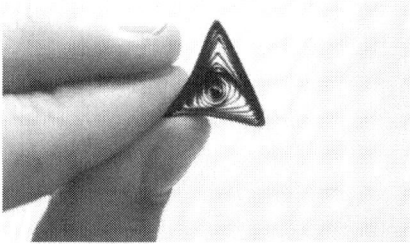

Once again, try both to see what works best for you.

**Triangle Variation**

To create a shape that resembles a shark fin, press in two sides of your triangle and leave the third side flat.

**Arrow**

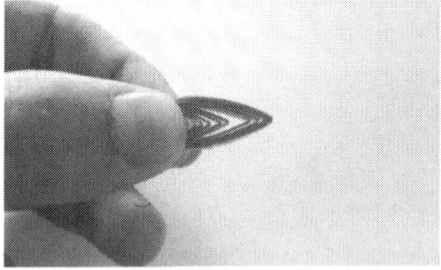

Make a teardrop, then pull the center down towards the base and hold it in place with your fingers.

# The Amazing Quilling Projects

Using the long side of the slotted needle, press down deeply into the base.

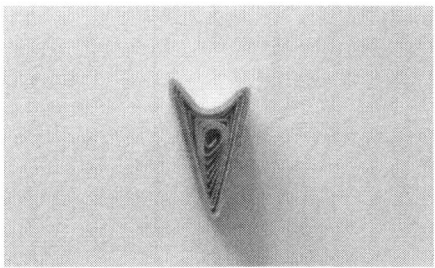

Release the tool and smooth the curve out with your fingers to shape.

**Arrowhead**

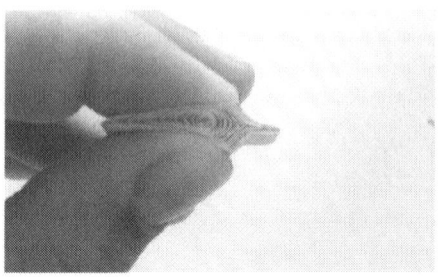

Beginning with a teardrop shape, hold the pointed end in your non-dominant hand and pinch the base end into a tight point.

Without letting go, slide your fingers down to meet the fingers of your opposite hand to create the side angles.

**Heart**

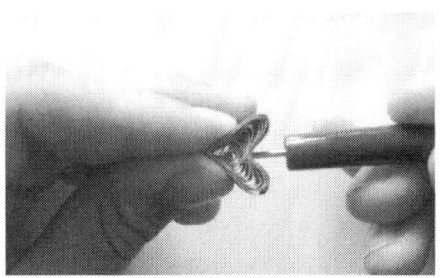

Once again, begin with a teardrop. Press in the base of the shape by using the point of your quilling tool to make a small indentation.

Release the tool and carefully press in each side of the heart to complete the center crease.

**Pentagon and Star**

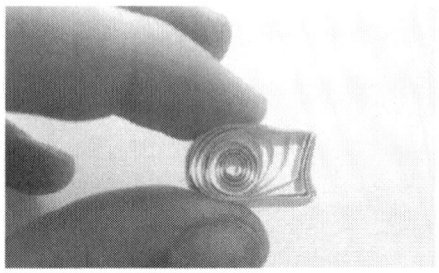

To make a pentagon, first create an elongated semi-circle as shown above.

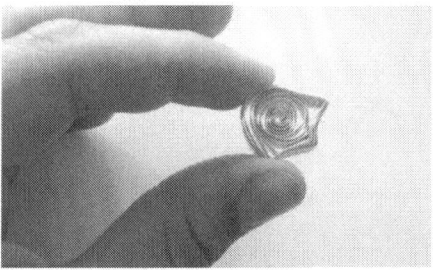

Pinch the center of the flat side using the same method you used when making the tulip shape; this is the peak of your pentagon.

Keeping the peak in the center, square off the bottom with two equal pinches on either side.

To turn the pentagon into a star, press in on each flat surface with your fingers or a quilling tool and then further refine each angle into peaks.

**Holly Leaf**

This shape is far and away the most difficult to create. For sanity's sake, you'll want to become comfortable making all of the other shapes before attempting this one!

Begin by making a marquis. Insert a set of tweezers into the shape; try to grip only about a third of the inside coil.

Keeping the grip with your tweezers, turn the marquis as needed and pinch a small point on either side of each peak.

You could also make the holly leaf by first making a square, adding a point to each end and then shaping all the angles into peaks.

# 5 Paper Quilling Patterns for Beginners

## Paper Quilled Monogram

**Supplies Needed:**

- ❖ Cardstock or precut quilling strips in desired colors
- ❖ A thick sheet of cardstock or board to use as the background
- ❖ A sheet of Cardstock for background
- ❖ Scissors
- ❖ Craft paper trimmer
- ❖ Mod Podge or tacky glue
- ❖ small-sized paintbrush

- Paper Plate or old plastic container
- Tweezers
- Shadowbox Picture Frame

**Print Your Outline**

1. Print your letter of choice in a light gray color onto the cardstock background.
2. An alternative method is to print the letter filled with black onto a sheet of paper, and then place the black letter print behind the piece of paper you plan to use as the monogram background. Place both sheets against a window and trace the letter with a pencil by hand onto the cardstock background. Make straight lines with a ruler and pencil tracing over the transfer pencil marks.
3. Erase any dark or stray pencil marks.

**Cut the Paper Strips**

1. Choose cardstock in colors you plan to incorporate into your design.
2. Cut one-quarter inch wide paper strips with a paper cutter from the colored cardstock.
3. You can buy precut quilling strips online or at the craft store if you want to skip this step. The choice is yours.

**Shape the Paper Strips**

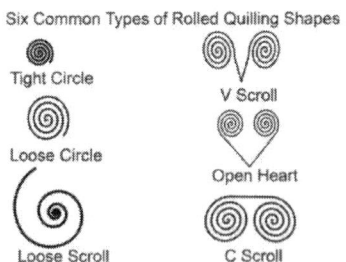

1. Decide what the design of the inside of your letter will be. It helps to look at photos for inspiration and make a preliminary quick thumbnail sketch for the layout of your monogram.

2. Make your shapes using a toothpick or quilling tool. Take your paper strip and wind it around your toothpick into the shape desired. Place a bit of glue onto the end of the paper strip to hold the shape in place. If you want a tighter more compact paper shape, roll it tightly. If you want a looser paper shape, roll it loosely.
3. It is a good idea to practice making different shapes until you get the hang of it. It takes some effort and patience to master the art of paper quilling, but if you are persistent, you will quickly be making lovely works of art.

**Glue the Quilled Paper Strips**

There is one important concept to remember when gluing your quilling strips: "Less is more" is the number one rule when it comes to gluing quilling strips to your baseboard. Too much glue can ruin your project, so be careful. Some people use a small brush to apply glue to the bottom of the quilling strips and then place and hold the strips onto the background until the paper pieces can stand up on their own.

Other people find that placing the quilling strips onto a paper plate with glue and then placing on the background works better for them. You have to practice and decide which method works for you.

Just remember to use a light touch when applying the adhesive to your paper strips.

**Frame the Outside of the Letter with Paper Strips**

The most important step of the quilled monogram process is to build a paper frame around your letter. Glue and place your strips, holding them until the glue is firm enough for the strip to stand up on its own. Make sure to have a one-quarter inch overlap on the ends of the paper strips, and secure the strips with a drop of glue. Allow the "wall" of your quilled monogram to dry thoroughly before proceeding to the next step.

**Start Filling in Your Letter Frame**

Once you have built your outside frame, it is time to fill in the insides of your monogram. Follow the design in your sketch and glue your shapes and strips into place. Allow the finished piece to dry completely for a few hours.

**Tweezers Are a Quillers Best Friend**

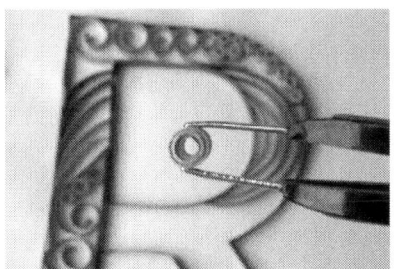

Tweezers are one of the most important tools you will use. It can be especially difficult to place quilled paper shapes into small spaces inside your quilled monogram project. Tweezers will go where your fingers cannot, saving you time and alleviating frustration.

**Frame the Finished Quilled Monogram**

After you have finished your project, you will want to place your quilled monogram into a frame. If you use a regular picture frame you will have to remove the protective glass from the front. There simply isn't enough room to allow for the raised surface of the quilled paper in a standard frame. If having the piece protected by the glass is important to you, you will find that a shadowbox frame will solve your problems. Shadowbox frames have an inch or more depth under the protective glass and are perfect to frame your quilled art piece.

This tutorial covers quilled alphabet letters, but you can do so much more with the art of quilling. You can make flowers, embellish cards and even make jewelry. If you love quilling, make sure to try other types of quilling projects and techniques. With time, practice and a little bit of patience, you will soon become a paper artist making beautiful works of paper art for yourself and your friends.

# Paper Quilled Teardrop Vase

What you willl need:

- ❖ A vase: I used a simply shaped bud vase in ceramic, which worked really well. You need an opaque vase, not too big, that has no extreme curves...only smooth and gentle curves.
- ❖ Paper strips in a gradient of colours: Search Ebay/Amazon or a paper craft shop and you'll find sets of paper strips sold cheaply in a vast array of colours. You'll only need one set for a small vase like mine.
(Or you can make your own if you have a guillotine.)
- ❖ Glue: Must be able to stick paper to ceramic. I used Aleene's tacky glue.
- ❖ Quilling slotted tool: This is a rod with a slot at the end basically and is cheap to buy.
- ❖ Quilling needle tool: You could use a cocktail stick instead, or anything with a point that can apply glue accurately.

❖ Quilling board (optional): Very handy to have so that you can make sure the teardrops are the same size. Could use a ruler instead though, or just draw a circle on a piece of paper to use as a guide!

*Handy to have*: Tweezers for moving fiddly items, and cotton buds to clear up stray glue.

**Step 1: Roll the Paper Spirals**

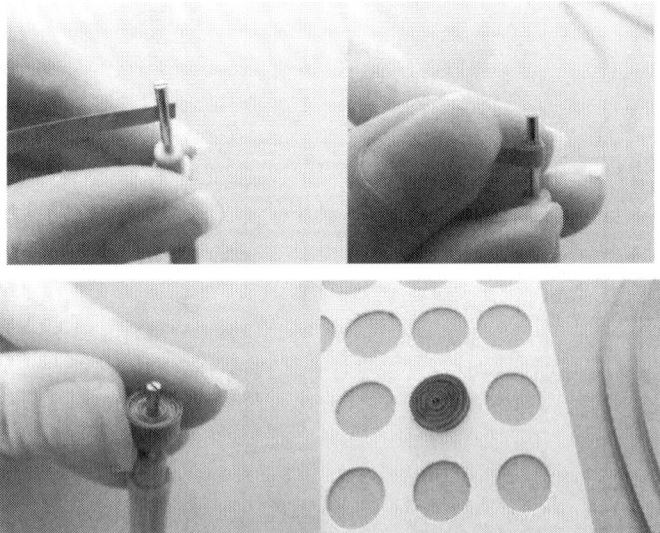

Starting with the darkest colour of paper you are going to use, put the very end of one paper strip into the slotted tool.

You want to rotate the tool whilst holding the paper strip so that the paper wraps tightly around the metal rod.

It's not vital, but the paper strips have one smoother side and one rougher side, so try and keep the smoother side on the outside of the spiral.

As you rotate the tool, keep the forming spiral resting on a finger to control it and keep it from becoming loose or getting into a mess.

Once you have made the whole strip into a coil, put the coil into a circle on the quilling board and let it slowly unfurl to fill the hole shaped guide. I used the third hole down which is 17mm across.

If you don't have a quillling board, you could use a drawn circle guide or a ruler and carefully let the coil become looser until it gets to the size you want.

Then you need to put a tiny bit of glue at the end of the paper strip, on the inside, to hold the coil in that shape. You can use a quilling needle or cocktail stick to apply the glue accurately.

**Step 2: Form the Teardrops**

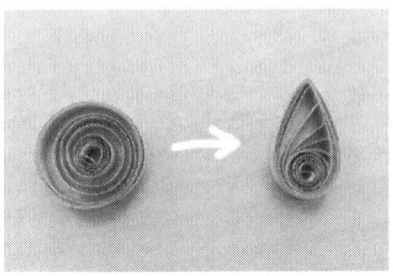

You need to take each of the coils you make and then turn them into teardrop shapes.

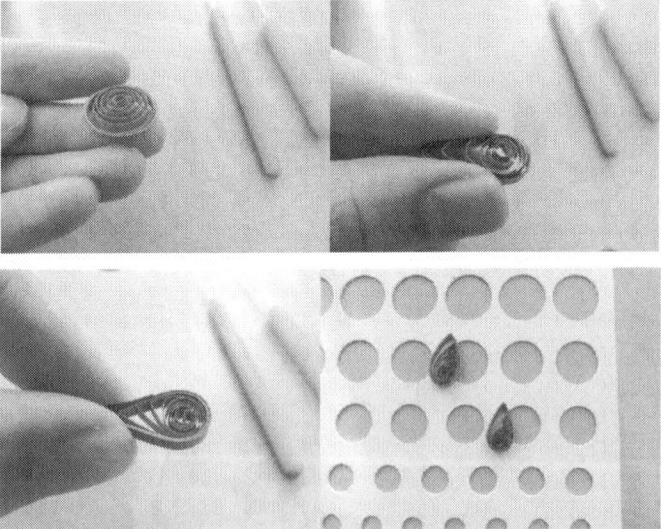

This is really easy and all you need to do is lightly squash half of the coil between your finger and thumb, and pinch one end to make a sharp fold.

It's up to your what sizes you make your teardrops and depends mostly on the size of your vase. I made 4 rows of one size and then made teardrops of a smaller size for the top row.

Step 3: Add the Teardrops to the Vase

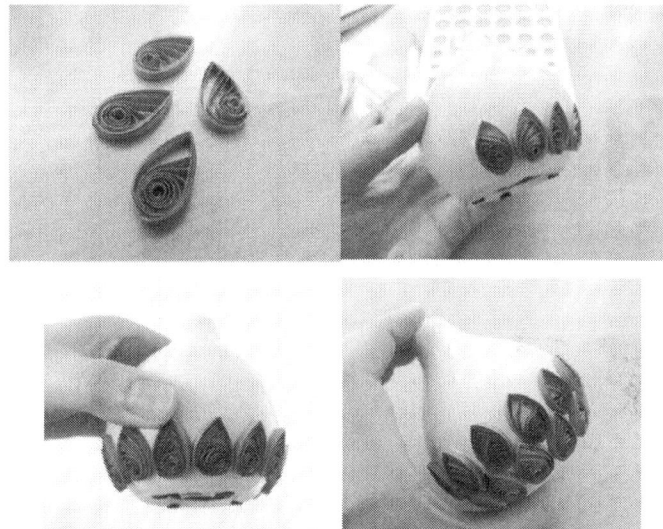

Make a handful of quilled teardrops to start you off. Then start gluing them to your vase, starting from the base.

Just apply a little glue to the back (mainly at the top and the bottom), and hold the teardrop onto the vase surface for a short while. It should stick pretty quickly.

Once you have completed one row, you can repeat all of the steps with a different colour and make the next row. And then just repeat this all of the way up your vase or until you want the design to finish.

I did 5 rows and stopped before the vase started to curve outwards at the top. Concave curves like that are hard to decorate but it can be done using smaller quilled shapes.

**Step 4: You have now finished your pretty quilled vase!**

# Paper Quilled Flower Cake

**Materials:**

- White printer paper
- Yellow paper
- Glue stick
- Scissors and/or paper cutter

# The Amazing Quilling Projects

**Instructions:**

1. For a fringed center, cut a small piece of yellow cardstock (1.5 cm X 3 cm) and fringe the edge. Roll it up and secure with a dab of glue
2. For the flower petals, cut 1/4" strips of printer paper.
3. Roll the strip into a tight coil, let it unroll a bit and secure with a dab of glue.
4. With two fingers, pinch the circular coil at the ends so the shape becomes more of a diamond.
5. Continue making the diamond shapes until you have enough petals.
6. To make a double-diamond petal, make two diamond coils and squish them together, securing them by wrapping another strip of paper around the outer edge of the two pieces and gluing in place.
7. Glue all your finished petals around the fringed or coiled center piece.

Now take your quilled flowers in addition to some kumquat branches or other foliage, and adorn your cake!

## Paper Quilling Flower Pendant

**What you need:**

- ❖ Quilling paper strips
- ❖ Glue
- ❖ quilling slotted tool
- ❖ 4mm faux pearl bead (optional)
- ❖ Jump ring
- ❖ Finished chain or cord
- ❖ Optional: additional beads to embellish chain

**How to make**

1. Select a paper strip in your first color, and use the slotted quilling tool to coil the strip.

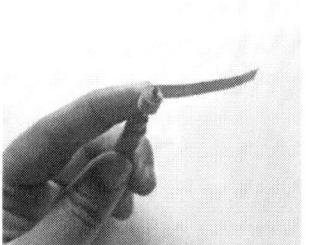

2. After coiling the entire strip carefully take it out of the quilling tool, holding the strip so that it doesn't uncoil.

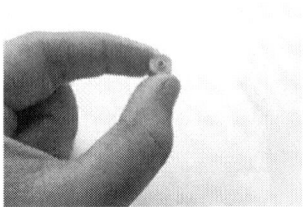

3. Allow the coil to loosen up a bit.

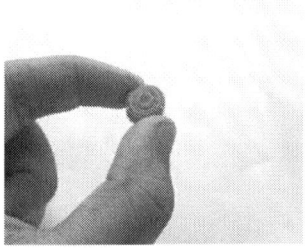

4. Place the loosely coiled strip on a flat surface and glue a small bead in the center of the quilled circle (optional).

5. Tighten the coil again by holding it between 2 fingers and pulling the open end. Once the center part has tightened, roll the rest of the strip around it and apply glue at the tip to secure your coil. This will be the center of the paper quilling flower.

6. Select a quilling strip in your second color and quill it using the slotted quilling tool.

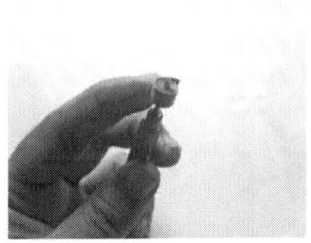

7. After quilling the strip carefully take it out of the tool.

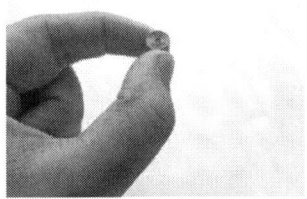

8. Allow the coil to loosen up a bit by placing it on a flat surface.

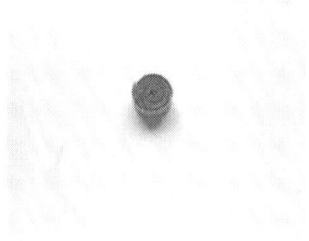

9. Take the loosely quilled pattern and pinch one side to create a pointy edge. You now have a teardrop shape.

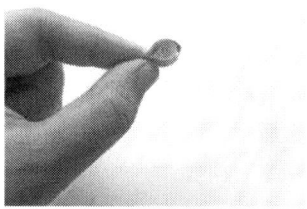

10. Now pinch the opposite side of the quilled strip to create another pointy edge. You now have an eye shape.

11. Repeat steps 6-10 to create 5 more eye shapes using the same colored strips for a total of six. Create 3 more eye shapes in your third paper color.

12. Take a piece of paper or plastic with a smooth surface (so that you can easily remove glued pieces). Place the center part of the flower on your surface. Take your first two eye shapes from your color that you have six of and attach them to the circle. Do this by gluing any of the pointy edges to the center circle. Glue the rounded part of the eye shapes to each other as well, connecting your petals.

13. Now take one from your second color of eye-shaped coils, and glue it the same way to the center and to the adjoining petal.

14. Repeat your pattern until your paper quilling flower shape is complete.

15. Create a tight coil with a relatively bigger loop on the center.

16. Attach the coil to the flower pattern between any two of your petals to serve as a loop. If you'd like to seal your design, now is the time to do so. Make sure you leave the hole in the coil that you created in step 15 open.

17. Attach a jump ring though the loop of the coil to complete the pendant.

18. Attach your jumpring to a cord or chain and wear with pride! If you'd like to add beads, you'll need to either finish your own chain, or remove the ends that came with it and choose large holed beads as accents.

Wear it and be proud of your paper quilling flower skills!

# Create A Quilled Paper Flower Photo Frame!

**What you need**

- ❖ Foam board
- ❖ X-acto knife and scissor
- ❖ Strong adhesive glue and craft glue
- ❖ Pencil and ruler
- ❖ Quilling paper
- ❖ Beads.

**Instructions**

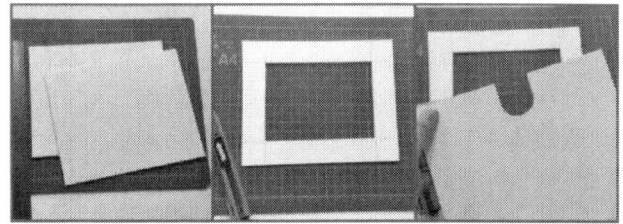

**Step-1**: Measure your photo size and cut out 2 pieces of foam board adding extra 2 inches on both width and length of the photo size. Draw 1 inch border around any one piece and an upside down arch shape right in the top middle part of the other piece. See the picture. Cut out the frame (the piece with borders) as neatly as possible. Cut out the arch shape neatly as well.

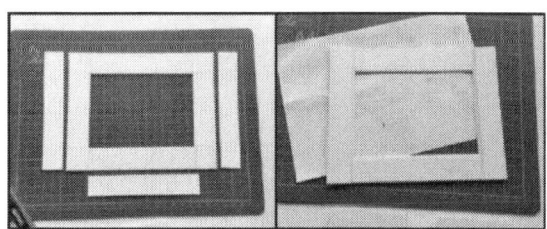

**Step-2**: Now place the frame on a plain surface. Measure and cut 3 pieces from the foam board for the sides and bottom part of the foam. Glue the pieces neatly along their place. The top side of the frame should remain open. This is for inserting the photo into the frame.

# The Amazing Quilling Projects

**Step-3**: Cut out a tie shaped pattern from the foam board for the stand. Make a half cut along the top 1.5 cm of the stand and bend it. Glue the back side of the frame and then glue the 1.5 cm part of the stand on the back side diagonally by keeping the corner matched with the corner of the frame.

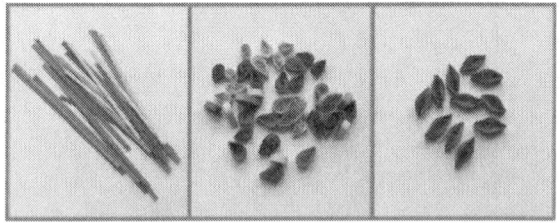

**Step-4**: Prepare papers strips for qulling. Use bright colors for the flowers and green for the leaves. Use the bright colored paper strips to make teardrop shaped pattern. Make as many as you need to create flowers. Use the green colored paper strips to make leaf shaped pattern. Make as many as you need.

**Step-5**: Place a scrap paper under the frame before starting the paper quilling art on the frame. Use white / craft glue to attach the quilled papers. Start to glue the quilled papers from a corner of the frame. Simply glue and place them. I used 6 teardrop pattern for each flower. You may add more petals if you want to. Glue more patterns to make a chain of flowers.

**Step-6**: Create more paper quilling flowers all around the frame. Try to keep a nice color combination. Glue the leaves between the flowers. I also added some faux pearl beads on the center of the flowers and some loose quilled circles in the small gaps.

# The Amazing Quilling Projects

Printed in Great Britain
by Amazon

74405615R00050